Eco Alert!
CLIMATE CHANGE

Rebecca Hunter

SEA-TO-SEA
Mankato Collingwood London

This edition first published in 2012 by

Sea-to-Sea Publications
Distributed by Black Rabbit Books
P.O. Box 3263, Mankato, Minnesota 56002

9 8 7 6 5 4 3 2

Published by arrangement with the Watts Publishing Group Ltd, London.

Library of Congress Cataloging-in-Publication Data

Hunter, Rebecca, 1935-
 Climate change / by Rebecca Hunter.
    p. cm. -- (Eco alert)
 Includes index.
 ISBN 978-1-59771-295-8 (library binding)
 1. Climatic changes--Juvenile literature. I. Title.
 QC903.15.H86 2012
 551.6--dc22

                              2011001189

Planning and production by
Discovery Books Limited
Managing Editor: Rachel Tisdale
Editor: Rebecca Hunter
Design: Blink Media
Picture Research: Colleen Ruck
Illustrations: Stefan Chabluk

February 2011
RD/6000006415/001

Photographs: **Alamy:** page 17 (Sigrid Dauth); **Ancient Art & Architecture Collection Ltd.**: page 8 (C. M. Dixon); **FEMA:** page 26 (Mark Wolfe); **Frank Lane Picture Agency**: page 25 top (Michael & Patricia Fogden/Minden Pictures); **Getty Images:** page 4 (CARL DE SOUZA/AFP), page 5 bottom (TORSTEN BLACKWOOD/AFP), page 13 (VIN MORGAN/AFP), page 19 (Travel Ink), page 20 (Dejan Patic), page 21 (KAMBOU SIA/AFP), page 23 bottom (LIONEL HEALING/AFP), page 27 bottom (Andrew Nelmerm), page 29 (Alex Wong); **Istockphoto.com**: cover (Phil Dickson), page 24 (Irving N Saperstein); **NASA:** page 5 top (GOES 12 Satellite); **Shutterstock:** page 7 (Dark o), page 9 (gary718), page 11 (Galyna Andrushko), page 15 (Konstantin Sutyagin), page 16 (Leksele), page 18 (Vladimir Melnik), page 22 (Sam Dcruz), page 23 top (Donald R Swartz), page 25 bottom (Susan Flashman), page 27 top (Wade H Massie).

Contents

Extreme Weather

What is happening to the world's weather? From all parts of the globe, reports are coming in of strange weather events that have never happened before.

On August 16, 2004, the villages of Boscastle and Crackington Haven in Cornwall, in England, experienced flash floods. Torrential rainfall (1 inch [24 mm] in just 15 minutes) led to a 6-foot (2-m) rise in river levels in an hour. A 10-foot (3-m) wave traveling almost 10 mph (16 km/h) surged down the main road, wrecking stores and houses, uprooting trees, and carrying cars out to sea.

⊙ A heap of cars in the village of Boscastle in Cornwall, after the flood in August 2004.

Hurricane Katrina was one of the five deadliest hurricanes in the history of the United States. The hurricane formed over the Bahamas, crossed Florida, and then strengthened rapidly over the Gulf of Mexico. On the morning of August 29, 2005, Katrina hit New Orleans, flooding more than 80 percent of the city. Its wind speeds reached 175 mph (280 km/h) and at least 1,830 people lost their lives.

⊙ Hurricane Katrina swirls over the Gulf of Mexico shortly before hitting the southern coast of the U.S. on August 29, 2005.

In February 2009, wildfires swept through the state of Victoria in southern Australia, destroying entire towns. More than 1,800 houses were burned down, leaving 7,000 people homeless. The fires caused such extensive damage because the land was very dry following a week of unusual, extremely hot weather. Daily temperatures had been almost 115°F (45°C) every day of the preceding week, and even the nighttime temperatures never dropped below 86°F (30°C).

Extreme weather events like these have always occurred from time to time. But many places now seem to be experiencing them on a more regular basis; some areas are hotter; some are drier; the storms are much stronger; the rain more torrential. Is the world's climate actually changing? Why is it happening and what can we do about it?

▶ Firefighters battle with bushfires in southern Victoria in Australia in February 2009.

What Is Climate?

Climate is the average weather in a place over a long period of time. Many things combine to create the climate of a place: how much sunshine it gets; how close to the **equator** it is; how high it is; and how close to the sea. Air, ice, water, and even living things all play a part.

The Climate System

The movement of heat and water around the air, water, and land is called the climate system. It starts with the Sun warming the Earth, which then warms the **atmosphere**. The atmosphere keeps the Earth from becoming too hot or too cold. Water is constantly moving between the land and the atmosphere. It **evaporates** from the oceans, lakes, and rivers and forms clouds, and returns to the ground as rain, snow, or hail.

The atmosphere keeps the Earth from becoming too hot or too cold.

The Sun heats the oceans and land.

The Earth gives out heat as the Sun warms it up.

Ice sheets, snow, and sea ice reflect sunlight.

Water evaporates, then falls as rain, snow, or hail.

Climate Zones

The surface of the Earth can be divided into different zones, or **biomes**, depending on what climate it has. Between the Tropic of Cancer and the Tropic of Capricorn is an area known as the **tropics**. Climates here can be hot and wet, as in tropical rain forests, or hot and dry, as in the Sahara Desert.

As you go farther away from the Equator, the climate gets cooler. These areas have **temperate** climates, characterized by grasslands and forests. For example, the **taiga** biome stretches across a large part of Canada, Europe, and Asia. It consists of mainly coniferous forests. In this biome, summers are short and mild, and the winters are long, cold, and dry. The areas around the North and South Poles have frozen polar climates. Although they can be very sunny in summer, the temperature never rises above freezing.

Tropic of
Cancer

Equator

Tropic of
Capricorn

The Human Effect

Many factors can cause the Earth's climate to change. Usually these changes take place over thousands of years. Today, scientists believe that the actions of humans are causing our climate to alter in a much faster way. Before we can consider if this is true, we need to look at how the Earth's climate has changed in the past, and the natural causes of climate change.

⊙ The savannah biome covers much of central Africa. It consists of grasslands with bushes and low trees.

History of Earth's Climate

I n the past the climate on Earth was sometimes very different to that of today. At times it was much hotter, at others, much colder.

In the Jurassic period, more than 100 million years ago, average temperatures were about 104°F (40°C)—compared to 59°F (15°C) today—and dinosaurs roamed the planet. During the last ice age, 18,000 years ago, nearly half the Earth was frozen and animals, such as saber-tooth tigers and woolly mammoths, lived in Europe and North America. Different types of evidence show us what past climates were like.

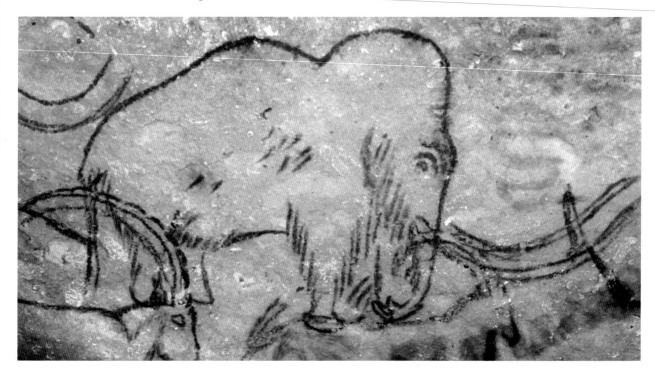

Documentary Evidence

Any writing or drawings left behind by people is known as documentary evidence. Stone Age paintings in caves in the Sahara Desert show that during the Ice Age, temperatures were much cooler there. The "Little Ice Age" was a period of cooling around the time of the seventeenth century. We know about this from written records and paintings from this time.

⊙ Cave paintings, such as this depiction of a mammoth in the Rouffignac Cave, in France, can tell us what the climate was like in this area more then 10,000 years ago.

Rocky Evidence

By looking at the layers in **sedimentary** rock, we can find out what the climate was like when they were formed, and learn about the plants and animals that lived then. Coal forms over millions of years in hot, tropical swamps. The **fossilized** remains of ancient plants and animals suggest the sort of climates that they must have lived in. Deep beneath Illinois and Kentucky are the fossilized remains of a huge tropical rain forest that existed more than 300 million years ago.

⊙ The rocks in the Grand Canyon, in Arizona, allow us to look back at more than 20 million years of geological history.

What Causes Climate Change?

E arth's current climate is the result of many forces that have been at work since the planet was formed more than 4 billion years ago.

The Greenhouse Effect

The Earth is heated by solar energy from the Sun. Much of this solar heat is absorbed by the land and water on Earth. Some of it is reflected back into space by clouds, gases, and the Earth's surface. A small number of gases are able to trap heat around the Earth. This trapping of heat is called the greenhouse effect because it works in the same way as a greenhouse. Thanks to the greenhouse effect, the Earth has a climate that is warm enough for us to live in.

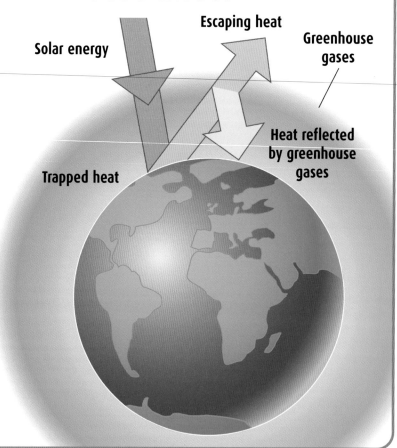

Solar energy

Escaping heat

Greenhouse gases

Heat reflected by greenhouse gases

Trapped heat

Sunspots

Sunspots are dark areas on the surface of the Sun that appear regularly. They reach a peak about every 11 years. At present, they show that the Sun is the coolest it has been for nearly 100 years. Some scientists believe that extremes of temperatures on Earth may be linked to the sunspot cycle.

Volcanoes and Meteorites

If there is an increase in dust and gas in the atmosphere, the Sun can be blocked out for weeks, months, or even years, leading to a change in climate. Many people believe that the mass **extinction** of animals—including the dinosaurs—65 million years ago, was caused by a giant **meteorite** hitting the Earth. The meteorite's estimated size was about 6 miles (10 km) in diameter. The dust and particles thrown upward when the meteorite hit Earth would have blocked the Sun's light for many years.

Volcanic eruptions can also cause cooler weather. The eruption in 1991 of Mount Pinatubo, in the Philippines, led to a decrease in average world temperatures of almost 2°F (1°C) for the next two years.

All these background forces have combined to help form our present climate. But is there now another force at work today? Are the actions of humans altering our climate, too?

Feedback Systems

Ice reflects sunlight well. The more ice there is on Earth, the more heat is reflected back into space. This keeps the planet cool, so more ice can form and more heat can be reflected. This is a type of feedback system, and it gets this name because the effect of an action "feeds back" and affects the cause.

Global Warming

The gases in the atmosphere that keep the Earth warm are known as greenhouse gases. They include carbon dioxide (CO_2), methane, nitrous oxide, ozone, and water vapor.

Many of these gases are produced by human activities, in industrial processes, by our homes, and by all forms of transportation. If enough of these polluting gases are added to the atmosphere, the greenhouse effect will increase, causing temperatures to rise. This is called global warming and it affects every country in the world.

Carbon Dioxide

Carbon dioxide is a very effective greenhouse gas that makes up only 0.03 percent of the atmosphere. When **fossil fuels** are burned in power plants, large amounts of CO_2 are released into the atmosphere and its levels are now rising rapidly.

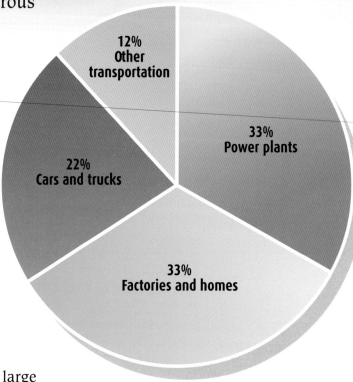

12% Other transportation

33% Power plants

22% Cars and trucks

33% Factories and homes

⊙ This pie chart shows where the extra CO_2 in our atmosphere comes from.

ENERGY SAVING STORE

Lighting and temperature levels are reduced to share in our community's efforts to reduce global warming

Ice Core Samples

The amount of CO_2 in past atmospheres can be measured from ice-core samples. These studies have shown that for most of the last 650,000 years the level of CO_2 in the atmosphere has always been below 300 parts per million (ppm). The level of CO_2 today has risen to 370ppm. This recent increase in CO_2 has been mirrored by a rise in average world temperature. This has risen by more than 1.08°F (0.6°C) since the 1850s. If this rise continues, some estimate that temperatures could increase by more than 9°F (5°C) by the end of the twenty-first century.

Scientists can drill into polar ice and take samples of ice dating back hundreds of thousands of years. Looking at the gases trapped in these samples and comparing them to the air in the atmosphere today gives them an idea of the climate in previous years. This enables them to measure the effects of global warming.

Carbon Footprint

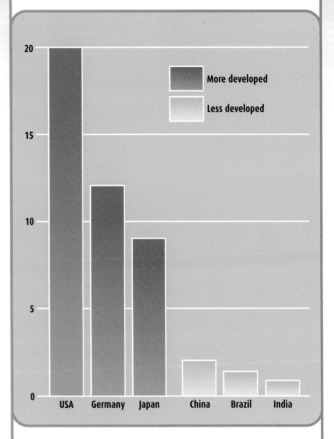

A carbon footprint is a measure of the amount of CO_2 produced by a person, organization, or country in a given time. Industrialized countries have much higher carbon footprints than those in developing ones.

How can you help?

Figure out your carbon footprint (see page 31) and then try and reduce it. You could walk or cycle more to reduce car trips, and take vacations locally to reduce air flights. Or plant a tree—a large tree will absorb approximately 44 lb. (20 kg) of CO_2 per year.

Oceans and Climate

Oceans play several important roles in controlling world climate. If their temperatures were to rise with global warming, there would be many consequences.

Global Climate

The oceans store more than 90 percent of the heat in the Earth's climate system. The climate of the world is influenced when warm water moves from the tropical regions toward the poles. Warm currents move water near the surface of the oceans, while cold currents are very deep. In this way the waters of the Pacific, Atlantic, and Indian Oceans are mixed, helping to control the climates of the nearby land.

▶ This map shows the major water currents in the world. The warm currents move in the surface waters (red), while the cold currents (blue) are at the bottom of the ocean.

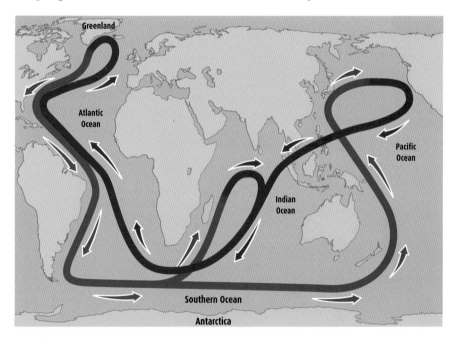

Greenland

Atlantic Ocean

Pacific Ocean

Indian Ocean

Southern Ocean

Antarctica

Carbon Sinks

A carbon sink is a place that collects and stores carbon. Oceans are natural carbon sinks, and store the largest amount of CO_2 on Earth. The CO_2 is **dissolved** into the water and then can be stored both in the water and in the bodies of sea plants and animals. About 93 percent of the CO_2 in the world is found in the oceans.

HOT SPOT:

El Niño

El Niño is a pattern of weather in the tropical Pacific that occurs every 3–7 years and causes the temperature of an area of the Pacific Ocean to rise by 3.6–5.4 °F (2–3°C). This changes rainfall patterns around the globe, causing heavy rain in the southern U.S. and severe drought in Australia. Scientists believe increasing CO_2 levels are making El Niño events more severe and more frequent.

Warming Up the Oceans

Cold water can absorb more CO_2 than warm water. This means that if the oceans warm up they will hold less CO_2. It is thought that oceans may remove up to 85 percent of the CO_2 that we are releasing into the air, but some oceans, such as the Southern Ocean, have already reached their **saturation** point and can absorb no more. The warming of oceans will also alter the currents, changing weather all over the world.

⊙ As well as helping control global climate, oceans are also the primary supplier of water to the atmosphere. This is then distributed over the Earth as rain, snow, or hail.

15

Ice Caps and Glaciers

About 80 percent of the Earth's fresh water is frozen. The North and South Poles are covered in ice, and more is found in icebergs, glaciers, and the snow and ice on mountain tops. If the world gets warmer, these icy areas will start melting.

Arctic Ice

The ice in the Arctic consists of a floating **ice cap** over the North Pole, and an **ice sheet** that covers most of Greenland.

An international team of scientists has been studying the rate that ice is melting in Greenland and has confirmed that recent warm summers have caused the most extreme Greenland ice melting in 50 years.

Each year in the summer in the Arctic, the edges of the ice sheet melt and retreat. The last six years have had the six lowest extents of ice. The ice is melting more quickly now than ever before.

Antarctic Melting

The Antarctic ice sheet is the largest mass of ice on Earth. It covers an area of almost 5.4 million square miles (14 million square km), and contains 7 million cubic miles (30 million cubic km) of ice. At present, scientists are worried about the melting of the West Antarctic ice sheet. While icebergs have always naturally broken away from the mainland, collapses of large areas of ice are happening more often.

In 2002, the Larsen B **ice shelf** in Antarctica collapsed and disappeared in just 35 days, when it was expected to last at least 100 years. If the West Antarctic ice sheet melted completely it would raise sea levels by 16 feet (5 m), flooding many coastal regions around the world. However, some scientists predict that it would take more than 1,000 years to melt this amount of ice.

Retreating Glaciers

Glaciers are formed in the mountains when snow is collected and compressed over many thousands of years. The melting of glaciers is a natural process and the meltwater is usually replaced by fresh snow. In the last 100 years, many glaciers have been melting at a faster rate than they are being replenished. If this continues, the glaciers will keep shrinking until they finally disappear.

How can you help?

Talk to your parents about changing their energy supplier to one that uses some form of **renewable energy**, not a fossil fuel energy source.

◀ This photograph shows the Rhone glacier, in Switzerland, which has retreated 1.5 miles (2.5 km) in the last 150 years.

Sea Levels

Sea levels are thought to have risen between 4–8 inches (10–20 cm) in the last 100 years. If global warming continues at the current rate they will rise even more. There are two things that cause sea levels to rise: **thermal expansion** and ice melt.

Thermal Expansion

When water is warmed up, it expands and takes up more space. So when oceans are warmed, they take up more space. The effect of this is that sea levels rise. Thermal expansion is currently the primary cause of sea level rise and is expected to remain so over the next century.

⊙ The highest point on the Maldive Islands is only 8 feet (2.4 m) above sea level. Even a very small rise in the sea level would submerge most, or all, of the islands, making 300,000 people homeless.

Ice Melt

Although it is worrying that ice shelves are melting, they are composed of floating sea ice, which does not contribute to sea-level rise. Just as a melting ice cube in a glass of water will not cause the water level in the glass to rise, sea ice will not raise the level of the sea when it melts. Only land-based ice melt will cause sea levels to rise.

Effects of Sea Level Rise

Predictions say that sea levels will rise 20 inches (50 cm) in the next 50 years. As the sea level rises, many low-lying islands may disappear completely under the sea. Many major cities are on the coast, and a sea-level rise of even 20 inches (50 cm) would flood so much land that half a billion people could be made homeless.

HOT SPOT:

The Jakobshavn Glacier

The Jakobshavn glacier in Greenland (above) is the world's fastest-moving glacier. Its speed has doubled in the last 20 years and it is now moving at 7.5 miles (12 km) a year. About 35 billion tons of ice is lost into the sea each year, which is thought to be responsible for 4 percent of sea-level rise.

Shifting Weather Patterns

One effect of climate change will be to change weather patterns all around the world. This will be good for a number of populations because some areas will become more habitable, but it will also be bad for many people.

Benefits of Global Warming

Satellite measurements now show that our planet is greener than it was before the onset of global warming. The rising CO_2 concentrations in the atmosphere have encouraged plants to grow more. The warmer weather also means a longer growing season. These factors combined mean that many areas have seen an increase in overall global food production.

In 2006 the UK's first commercial olive grove was planted in Devon, in southwestern England. Temperatures have risen enough in recent years to make it possible to grow this Mediterranean plant in England.

How can you help?

▶ Save energy by turning off lights and any electric machines not in use.

▶ Turn off your computer— don't leave it on standby.

▶ Turn your heating down or your air-conditioning up by 2°F (1°C).

Hotter and Drier

Sadly, for every place that sees benefits of global warming there will be others that suffer. Many areas that are already semidry, such as many parts of Africa, will become too hot or too dry to grow crops. They will experience droughts that could turn the land to desert. Countries with temperate climates are likely to suffer both floods and drought at different times of year.

More Hurricanes

Hurricanes form over oceans that are warmer than 79°F (26°C). As the oceans warm up, more hurricanes are likely to happen. They may occur in places where they have never been seen before. Some experts predict that in the next century hurricanes may be up to 20 percent stronger than today.

⊚ Severe flooding is already causing problems in many countries. Most **climate models** predict even more flooding in the future. These people in Abidjan, Ivory Coast, suffer regularly from severe flooding. They hope their houses will be relocated in the near future.

Freshwater Resources

If global warming continues, water resources around the planet will be redistributed. Some areas that currently have enough water will dry up because of droughts; others will have too much water, leading to flooding and **erosion**.

Himalayan Glaciers

The glaciers in the Himalaya mountains of Asia are melting fast. The Himalayas contain the largest store of water outside the polar ice caps and feed seven large Asian rivers. The melting of the glaciers will first cause flooding and then drought. This will lead to huge environmental problems for hundreds of millions of people in China, Nepal, and India who rely on the water for drinking and for **irrigating** their crops.

⊙ The snow and ice in the glaciers of the Himalayas supply 40 percent of the world's population with water.

HOT SPOT:

Losing Lake Mead?

A recent study has shown that Lake Mead (above), on the Colorado River, could dry out by 2021, due to increased evaporation caused by global warming and a predicted long period of drought. The lake currently supplies water and **hydroelectric** power to more than 22 million people.

Rainfall Patterns

Rising temperatures around the world will lead to increased evaporation from the oceans and an increase in rainfall. Unfortunately, this is unlikely to be spread evenly across the world. Some areas will receive much more rain; others will dry out. These changes in rainfall will considerably affect the water available for human consumption, agriculture, and energy generation across the world.

◀ Women in the Democratic Republic of the Congo begin their daily trek for drinking water. By 2020, it is expected that between 75 and 250 million people in Africa will be suffering water shortages.

Effects on Wildlife

The effects of climate change aren't restricted to humans. Plants and animals are under threat as climate change alters their **habitats**. Some species will find things change for the better as new habitats open up for them. Others may not be able to **adapt** or move quickly enough and so may not survive.

Loss of Arctic Ice

Diminishing sea ice in the Arctic might make life difficult for polar bears. The bears hunt seals from the ice and if this disappeared, they would have to swim farther to find icebergs to rest on. The polar bear may be in danger in the future, but there are thought to be at least 25,000 in the Arctic today.

▶ A polar bear hunts for food from the Arctic sea ice.

24

The golden toad of Costa Rica (left) is thought to be extinct as a result of global warming. The forests of Costa Rica are now less misty due to the warming of the oceans and the atmosphere. This has led to an increase of fungal infections, which damage the moist skins of frogs, toads, and salamanders.

Changing Bird Distributions

Climate change is already having an impact on European birds. Some birds are expected to do well as temperatures rise, but more will suffer. A recent survey has looked at the change in population of a number of bird species over the past 20 years. Of 122 species that were studied, only 30 have increased their range, while 92 species have reduced in numbers. Many birds' territories are expected to shift to the north as it gets warmer in the south.

How can you help?

Recycle as much plastic, glass, and paper as you can. Recycling one glass bottle causes 20 percent less air pollution and 50 percent less water pollution than when a new bottle is made.

◀ The little egret, a bird of Africa and India, was first spotted as far north as the UK in 1989 and is now seen frequently and known to be breeding in southern England.

25

The Skeptics

Not everyone agrees that climate change is being caused by human actions. People who disagree with a popular view are called skeptics, and the climate change issue has many.

Natural Causes

Some people think that Earth's climate is controlled by natural events and that we cannot cause the climate to change. For example, they argue that human contributions to greenhouse gases account for only about 0.3 percent of the greenhouse effect. About 99.7 percent is due to natural causes, mostly increased water vapor in the atmosphere, which we can do nothing at all about. Some skeptics think that human activity has little impact on climate change.

Mistaken Models

Other skeptics think that some of the information we are given is wrong. Many of the statistics given in this book are preceded by the words, "predictions say…" or "scientists expect…". These forecasts are often based on theories that do not always turn out as expected. Climate models say that if temperatures are increasing on Earth, they should increase all the way up through the atmosphere. But weather balloons and satellite readings show that the lower atmosphere is not warming up. The models appear to be wrong.

⊙ Some climate models predict that hurricanes are likely to increase in number and become stronger. But, despite storms such as Hurricane Katrina, records show that tropical hurricane activity is actually at its lowest for 30 years.

Predictions say that sea levels are expected to rise between 8 and 24 inches (20 and 60 cm) by the end of the century. At the moment, sea levels are continuing to rise at a steady rate of 0.11 inches (3 mm) a year, which is what they have been doing for the last 200 years. Sea levels have been rising generally since the end of the last ice age 18,000 years ago, long before humans could have had any effect.

◉ Eighty percent of the world's power comes from fossil fuels. Companies that produce electricity from fossil fuels, and the industries that use it, are eager to believe that burning fossil fuels doesn't have any effect on global warming.

◉ As the last Ice Age ended, the climate became warmer and mammoths found it hard to adapt to the change. The last mammoths died out about 11,000 years ago, victims of prehistoric global warming.

What Can We Do?

We may never know whether we are causing climate change. At present, most experts agree that global warming is happening and that it is caused by human activity. Whatever the true situation, we should still do what we can to avoid causing any future damage to our planet.

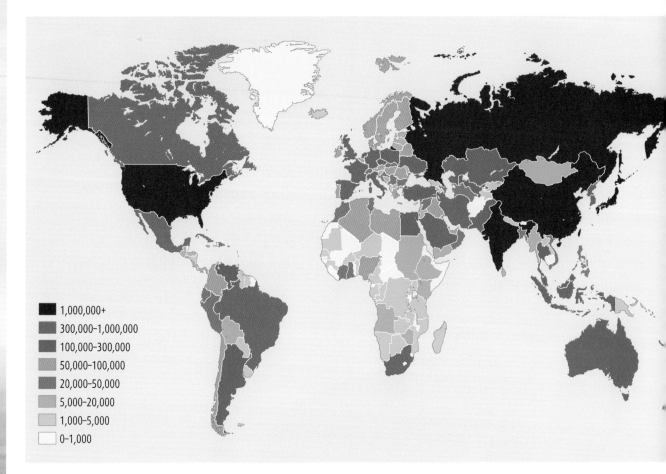

Legend:
- 1,000,000+
- 300,000–1,000,000
- 100,000–300,000
- 50,000–100,000
- 20,000–50,000
- 5,000–20,000
- 1,000–5,000
- 0–1,000

Reducing Carbon Dioxide Levels

The burning of fossil fuels produces around 20 billion tons of CO_2 per year. To reduce CO_2 levels in the atmosphere countries must rely less on fossil fuels and more on renewable resources, and **nuclear power**.

This map shows the amount of CO_2 produced by different countries, shown as tons of CO_2 per year.

Renewable Energy

Countries such as Switzerland and New Zealand, which have high mountains and rainfall, can use their natural resources to produce renewable hydroelectric power.

Solar power is another form of renewable energy. In Portugal, the world's largest solar power plant is being built. It will supply enough energy for 30,000 homes and will help prevent the emission of 86,500 tons of CO_2 a year from coal-fired power plants.

If only 4 percent of the world's desert areas were covered with solar panels, they could supply all of the world's electricity. The Gobi Desert alone could supply almost all of the world's total energy demand.

Young people demonstrate for urgent action on climate change and cleaner energy in the Power Shift rally in Washington, D.C., in March, 2009.

Earth Summit 2012

In 1992, more than 100 heads of state met in Rio de Janeiro, Brazil, to discuss urgent environmental problems. They signed the Climate Change Convention in which countries would try to reduce the level of greenhouse gases in the atmosphere to help stop global warming. Another Earth Summit meeting will be held 20 years later in 2012 in Brazil to see what has been achieved since then and to set a new course of action.

Glossary

Adapt
To change to suit different conditions.

Atmosphere
The layer of gases that surrounds the Earth.

Biome
A division of the world's vegetation that has a particular climate and has certain types of plants and animals.

Climate models
A computer-generated idea of what the climate will be like in the future based on current facts.

Dissolve
To become absorbed into a liquid solution.

Equator
The imaginary line around the middle of the Earth.

Erosion
The wearing away of rock or soil by the action of water or wind.

Evaporate
To change a liquid into a gas.

Extinction
The dying out of all members of a species.

Fossil fuels
Fuels including coal, oil, and natural gas that were formed underground millions of years ago.

Fossilize
When the remains of animals or plants are preserved in rock over million of years they are said to be fossilized and are known as fossils.

Habitat
The natural conditions in which a plant or animal lives.

Hydroelectricity
Electricity generated by the power of water.

Ice cap
A mass of ice and snow that spreads out from a center and permanently covers a large area of land.

Ice sheet
A large area of glacial ice.

Ice shelf
Part of an ice sheet that projects out to sea.

Irrigate
To supply water for growing crops.

Meteorite
A piece of rock that has reached the Earth from outer space.

Nuclear power
Power produced when atoms are split in a radioactive reaction.

Renewable energy
Energy that is obtained from sources that are renewable and will not run out.

Saturation
When something absorbs and holds onto so much of a substance that it can hold no more.

Sedimentary
Rocks that have been formed by material being deposited by water, wind, or ice. The materials are compacted into layers of rock.

Taiga
The subarctic coniferous forests of North America, northern Europe, and Asia.

Temperate
A climate that has a range of moderate temperatures.

Thermal expansion
The increase in volume as something is heated.

Tropics
The area of the world on either side of the equator and between the Tropics of Capricorn and Cancer.

Further Information

Books

Climate Change (World at Risk)
Andrew Solway, Franklin Watts, 2009

Climate Change (Global Viewpoints)
Adrienne Wilmoth Lerner and Chiara St. Pierre, Greenhaven Press, 2009

How We Know What We Know About Our Changing Climate:
Scientists and Kids Explore Global Warming (About Our Changing Climate)
Lynne Cherry, Dawn Publications, 2008

Changing Climate (Earth SOS)
Sally Morgan and Jenny Vaughan, Franklin Watts, 2007

Climate Change (Science in the News)
Chris Oxlade, Franklin Watts 2007

Web Sites

www.bioregional.com/our-vision/one-planet-living/
Calculate your carbon footprint and download a personal action plan showing
how you can reduce your impact on the environment.

www.epa.gov/climatechange/kids/index.html
The Environmental Protection Agency's site for kids focusing on the science
and impacts of global warming and on actions that help address climate change.

http://climate.nasa.gov/
NASA's Eyes on the Earth. Critical data on the rate and extent of global climate change.

www.greenpeace.org/international/
Up-to-date information on the climate change situation and what action
is being taken to tackle it.

Note to parents and teachers: Every effort has been made by the publishers to ensure that these web sites
are suitable for children and that they contain no inappropriate or offensive material. However, because of
the nature of the Internet, it is impossible to guarantee that the contents of these sites will not be altered.
We strongly advise that Internet access is supervised by a responsible adult.

Index